DEVOTION

POEMS BY
JONATHAN BYRD

FIRST EDITION
Copyright © 2021 by Jonathan Byrd
All Rights Reserved
ISBN-13: 978-1-7348692-5-5

Library of Congress Control Number: 2021930719

No part of this book may be performed, recorded, thieved, or otherwise transmitted without the written consent of the author and the permission of the publisher. However, portions of poems may be cited for book reviews—favorable or otherwise—without obtaining consent.

Cover Design: John Dixon

MEZCALITA PRESS, LLC
Norman, Oklahoma

For Kitten

CONTENTS

PROLOGUE
ATTENTION & DEVOTION ..... A
INVITATION ..... B
THE ONE AND HOLY WORD C

DEVOTION
I - C 1

ATTENTION & DEVOTION

In the absence of you,
books fill my bed.
I continue to devour you
through the night.

Every word is a child
of our deep longing
to know each other.

INVITATION

Okay, she said.
Let's get this over with
as slowly as possible.

THE ONE AND HOLY WORD

One morning in the spring I heard a hissing
I walked into the garden and stood listening
It seemed as if there was some sort of magnet,
a circuit humming, coming through the planet

The Sun was streaming, creaming in the blossoms,
the tongues of bees repeating in devotion
the anthem of the budding and the buzzes,
the one and Holy Word of God and Goddess

YES YES YES YES YES

I.

In the evening I took the train into Buxton.
The cabin lights, half-mirrored on the window,
shook as the train shook.

Beyond that illusion, a star gave birth
to a pinpoint of wonder in an ordinary night,
burning to death, curving space and time.

At long last, a message from you.
You are wearing a rose, waiting at the station
in an ocean of half-light.

The train shook. The star stood. Nothing on Earth mattered as much.

II.

My heart has been crushed like an apple in a press
and this is the sweet juice of that disaster.
I don't deserve it. Please take it from me.
I will drink water and watch you enjoy it.

I will tend the tree. I will live in the orchard.
I will intoxicate you with sunlight.
I will stack the old wood outside your door.
I will prune until there is only you.

I promise, when all this work is done,
I will come and knock at your three-windowed door,
bathed in sweat and smoke and a summer of longing,
and ask you for a glass of your sweet juice.

III.

I must have watched this video a thousand times.
You're blowing a dandelion at the camera.

It takes you five breaths:

The first one is casual and moves some from the bottom.
This is how I know you are playful.

The second breath is a failure and you laugh at it.
This is how I know you are resilient.

On the third and fourth, you get down to business.
This is how I know you are committed.

At the end, there is one seed. You look at the stem.
You turn the fairy's wing toward you.
You blow a tiny, focused breath.

You smile at the camera. The rest of my heart goes floating away.
This is how I know you will get what you want.

IV.

water makes paper and also destroys it
you transform me

water shapes the land and land holds the water
you communicate with me

water is unstoppable, and yet teachable
you offer yourself

Are you willing? I am willing.
I will control you. You will allow me.
Feel the rain. The mountains wash into the sea.

V.

This lesson you are teaching me:
I've heard it before.
I heard it in the words that weren't in the Bible.

I heard it in the singing tree tops,
in the cry of the hawk, who takes and does not ask,
in the rasp of the rabbit, made to be taken.

I heard it in the sad, quiet masturbation of a priest,
and in the pale creak of the belt around the neck
of the man who loved him.

I heard it outside my office window in the wild and murderous breath of wisteria
and in the hollow of regret, the walking ghost of a life never lived

I hear it in the whisper of fabric
as you take off your dress.
Over and over it says,
I never denied you.
I never denied you.

VI.

I knock on the front door of the temple,
then enter through the back.

The Devil is pinned to her bedsheets.
Even God is surprised.

VII.

Last night your breast was the color of moonlight.
I rose to meet you. You lifted me.
We breached the battery wall.
We destroyed the slave market.
We liberated the dead from their lonely graves.

Even now, they are rocking in the tide,
white bones in a winedark sea, so intertwined that,
to the untrained eye, they are indistinguishable.

VIII.

Even the church has gutters,
a place for the mind to wander.
Her perfume fills the sanctuary,
exalted above all perfumes.

I am a beast of the field.
I am a creeping thing that creepeth.
She is the divided waters.
She is the night and the day.

She is made for me.
She is made from me.
There are seven days until
we are back in this holy place,

this wretched place where we
cannot touch or even say these
profane, profound things.
God knows, so I tell Him:

Seven days is not enough, Lord.
Bring the fruit to my mouth.
Bring the clay to my hands.
Seven days is not enough.

IX.

We are attracted to each other because
we are in so many ways the same.
Suddenly we realize there's a part
of ourselves that we've never known.

Explore with me. Explore in me.
We need a map and the only way
to make one is to go there.
Put on your boots. We'll strip naked at the river.

This is where the blackberries are.
We will call this ridge The Spine.
We call this valley The Temple.
We enter on our hands and knees.

X.

I took my son to school this morning.
I found a guitar player for Saturday.
Now I am home working on a poem.
Later, I will go to yoga and then,
finally, I will see you again.

You can see already that this is not poetry.
These words are a flat map of the Earth,
not even a pale drawing of your fruitful hips.

Where do we put the magnitude of this longing?
Where does pain become pleasure?
Where are the wildest places, places a man
might lose himself and never come out?

Is anything else even real?

Shall we put the bed in the reading room?

There is a little brown fleck in the blue iris of your left eye.
That's where I'm going after yoga.

XI.

I am meeting you for lunch.
I am trembling in my office.
Where there is no light,
the shadows are a curiosity,
the sweet lovesickness
making a divinity of desire.

The moment is alive
with potential, able to track
the movement of beauty.
We are afraid of places.
Let's bring a guide.

Creation is union!
Is this lifeforce a sin?
Can a journey change your heart?

I want to be bad, slow
and senseless in the darkness,
the edge of secret energy,
making medicine and divinity
out of imagination.

The seductive Earth.
The fruit to share.
The evolution of trust.
Lover: the noble self within fear.

XII.

You don't have to earn my love, she said.
The bridges burned behind me: Revolution!
I'll take this town beginning with her bed,
if this is how she holds negotiations.

I say, Put your hands above your head.
I think I've made her come to this agreement.
Maybe she has planned this all instead
and, if so, a glorious achievement.

Nothing like a coup to make your morning,
her sleeping lashes: flags of her surrender.
The one who burns, the one who does the burning:
it's hard to say who really has the power.

You don't have to earn my love, she said.
You are mine, I whispered, and she sighed.

XIII.

Under a black oak, a dog runs back and forth on its chain. I'm stopped at a light. I check my phone to see if there are any messages from you.

The dog sniffs the air and barks. There's a whole world out there, just beyond where the dog-oiled dirt turns to grass. Somewhere, there's an easy meal. Somewhere, there's a bitch in heat.

A man sticks his head out the front door and yells, SHUT UP.

What a waste of breath.

I want you. I smell you. I need you. The world seems so big. From the end of a chain, any distance is infinite. You were right here in my truck a few days ago.

I touched your thigh. I owned the whole world.

XIV.

"This is so dirty," I said.

"No," she said. "This is normal."

I said, "This is normal."

She said, "Good boy."

XV.

The wild thing between us
meets my gaze.
There's no second-guessing
this desire.

The hair on my body
is standing.
Not fear- fascination.
Reverence.

The Queen of wilderness
invites me.
Her smell is a garden
grown over.

The water in her hair,
electric.
The smoke in her forest,
a warning.

She is not mine alone
forever.
If I go to her now,
I'll be one.

Here with the hares and hawks,
who know not
respect or forgiveness,
I take her.

I give to her, reckless,
emboldened,
An old song sung tuneless,
my voice raw.

Hear it ache over miles
and echo.
Someone has the Goddess
by her hair.

Poor chap, taken to feed
her children,
gayly he goes, singing his
warrior song.

XVI.

Last night, we gave each other gifts.
You made dinner. I sang songs.
Nothing seemed good enough.

You apologized for your food.
I apologized for my music.
That was the last straw.

I stormed your castle.
You captured and tortured me.
The ruins of Shame burned in the night.

We are learning from this beautiful war.
Show no mercy. Surrender completely.
No apologies.

XVII.

A. God comes sterile, a Universe of hydrogen and space black as a Bible. Have you been purified? Sanctified? Have you repented of your musky sin?

B. Eve was made of young goat skin and stuffed with wet moss. There were no high heels but, all the same, she pained herself and ignored the pain.

C. Every man was made of Eve and her musk, her boiled roots and tinctures. The fire was rust and water. Eve was two women, maybe more, like any woman.

D. Adam feared his wife- Adam, who named the wolf! God gave him a choice and Adam chose to follow Eve and serve as her King. Every day she was new.

E. The large things are simple. The largest is nothing. Her smell is everything, and so small. God, who set all things in motion? Her motion amazes even Him.

XVIII.

He desired her and she ran away.
He killed her and she returned.
He understood her and became a man.

XIX.

The magician holds up a raspberry.
She places it in her audience's hand.
Gently, she brings the hand to her lips.
Before his eyes, the fruit is transformed

into fire.

XX.

The water's silent,
not quiet but present,
attuned to you as a predator
where you stand,
life in your hands.

The water listens
to Hecate on her mission
crouching deeper still
in the grove of honeysuckle
dirt beneath your fingernails
as you will.

The waters move,
a child in love with the Beloved,
the flower of your lips
taking life in little sips,
the fertile circle of focus
the turtled curve of the locus
trellised through the ironwood.

XXI.

I feel like a man in a cage.
It's a mighty big cage, as
big as the whole world without you.

Wherever you aren't I am
looking out from a third story
window, hunting you with my scope.

I walk on my wheel. I get
stronger every day. I sleep
in chips and sniff the edges of if ever.

Inside the palm of your hand,
the head line deep, the heart
line long, the life line broken like

a jailhouse wire. Put me in
there. I'll bridge the circuit.
I'll arch in mad arcing sparks vi-

brating, eyes turning inward
as life flashes like lightning,
growing smaller until your heartbeat

is thunder, your head is the
Heavens, your life is a thou-
sand pages of the Bible, burning.

Then I'll be free in the little
box of your bed, the brittle
bowls of your eyes, keyholes to heaven.

XXII.

Our date began days before, when you sent me a picture of a dress,
your new dress, tied at the back of your neck,
a thin black bow that draped down the space
in the hole that showed the skin between your shoulder blades.

When you stepped up into my truck the black strands danced and dangled.

There were no tables available, so we sat at the bar.
You leaned in to take a bite of your food.
I placed my hand on your back. I fingered the black bellropes under my palm.

The play was starting soon. I paid for our food.
There was an urgency. I drove fast through the city streets.
I wanted to see the beginning.

I enjoyed the play. This time you sat on my left
and my left hand traced the silky black knot
as children grew and people died and nothing was ever the same again.

When the father tried to talk to his son about sex,
and then handed him a book instead, I cried.
I cried for the time I had no language for my desire,
someone who could say, This is what I want. Like this.
This is how I am made. Like this. Unmade, like this.
I hoped someday he would be able to speak as we have spoken,
to know the dark places, voices trembling, to speak
and speak until one thing could be unspoken.

Walking up the path to your door, I watched the last
of the little black straps dance across the skin of your back.
I looked up at Arcturus and Jupiter, surrounded by his lovers.
You said, "I really need to get into something more comfortable."

You stood in front of your mirror. You pulled your hair up.
You waited for me.

XXIII.

You laughed at the noises I made when I ate my salad.
You have asked me to teach you about food. Well.

I confess that I may not have made those noises alone,
sitting in a lunch cafe, finding a hotel, calling my agent.

But with you there, your fingernails the color of
sweet white Trebbiano grapes pressed and boiled
down to a dark syrup, aged in oak with the dark
and hungry little mothers of all life, aged twelve years
in smaller and smaller kegs made of chestnut,
cherry, ash, mulberry, and juniper, all adding their
character to this aceto balsamico tradizionale? Well.

The salad slowly revealed itself until there was nothing
but an orgy of sweet vinegar that I sopped with my finger.

XXIV.

crossing boundaries
out on the edge of ourselves
we find each other

XXV.

You asked me if your body was enough
for me. Of course it's not. That's why I'm back
here typing. Is the alphabet enough
to say it all? In carbon black, letters lack

the depth of flesh, my mouth so full of you
I cannot speak, the echo of your screams
inside the fibers of my pillow. Turn
around so we can finish up this scene.

I hate to waste the backside of a page.
I'll need another soon and maybe reams
and fingers made of glass to turn this rage
so gently that it fills another's dreams.

Enough? Well, hold your breath and think of this:
A breath is not enough, but breathing is.

XXVI.

She said, Use your finger.

I said, What's the magic word?

She said, Now.

XXVII.

She said, My name is Eve. Are you good or evil?

I said, I'm good.

She said, Oh. That means I get to be Evil.

XXVIII.

Freddie King is singing on the radio.
It's lonely when you're on your own.
You feel like a drowning man.

The mountains are breathing the wet breath of the Earth.
I have this picture of you with greenbrier across your face.

Wild daisies and golden ragwort strut right from the rocks.
Sumac feathers the mountainside.
Oh baby, Freddie says.

I want to fuck you to this record, swimming the breaststroke
while Freddie drowns in the blue blue sea.

I want to kiss you in the dripping woods behind your house.
Sweet honeysuckle crawls the trees and humps the fence line.

Mist rises from the back of the dragon.
The bass player fucks the drummer.
The horns shout hallelujah.

Hallelujah to the exquisite agony of the blues.
Hallelujah to the blue ridge of white pine and the dirty dirty clouds.

Your body is the Earth. Your body is the sky.
Your body is the blues. Your body is the drummer.
I'm playing bass.

XXIX.

You're surprised I still have sunlight. I'm in another time zone.
Sitting on the trees behind these rice fields, the big red Sun
doesn't seem to be ninety-three million miles away. Your voice sounds like
a lonely cashier at a drive thru. If only I could find the window.

How did the Earth find the Sun in this whole big Universe?
We were designed together. My blue eye. Your copper face.
Our hemisphere is falling asleep. The night sighs. The Earth turns.
The Sun spoons. Warmth spreads all down through Asia.

XXX.

You said I was a natural Switch.
I said, Yes Mistress, Thank you.
But when you whispered, "As you wish,"
then Daddy had to spank you.

XXXI.

I see a young woman on a train
in a blue hat with white netting.
Her hair is red.
Her eyes are lost.

A tall man, older than her,
watches her board from his seat
in the coffee car.
His hair is grey.
His eyes are firm.

He sees the way her blue skirt
binds her legs.
Her face is a garden of cream.

She sees him looking at her.
He doesn't smile, but there is
nothing cold about his not smiling,
his broad tweeded shoulders.

"Do you like poetry?" he says.

"So I wait for you like a lonely house," she says.

He smiles. "Neruda. Please." His palm turned upward.
"Sit with me," he says. "What are you reading?"

"Your mind," She says.

XXXII.

May twenty-fourth. I want to remember this holy number,
month and moon, your second cycle burning
like the fire you made, the blanket you laid that hid
the hole you dug to hold me while you went for
help. Help me, goddess. Help me, moonlight.

Feed him, she said. Show him the sky, the stars,
your eyes ambitious in scope, telescopes gathering
light from a spiral of vulnerable lights, a burning
of fusion, a coming together of masses in matchless
energy. Against all gravity, light says, Yes.

Speaking your fear to me, crushing the weight of resistance
against me, holding the headboard, head borne skyward
worshipping all the will that is not yours.
Don't say no to me, I said, and you shook Yes
into my breast, a heart of lips and blood like water,

eyes burning like Venus boiling, morning
and evening, both and neither like Yes and No
bonding, bound like hands above me binding
the day to the night, the borders of sense and senses.
No sense was in you. I was in you. You said,

No, a little girl napping, eyes clapping open
and shut, Yes holding my shirt and hiding.
Little big girl, let the moonlight in. I'll hold you.
You called her. You asked her what to do. She told you.
Burn, and blacken the edges of reason, seasons

pass through you sleeping, now awakened.
You said, I'm sorry, that was confusing. I said no.
I understood completely. You told me so sweetly, pulling
space around you. There I found you, light and dark
colliding, overriding. Maybe the day is not important.

But I want to remember this holy number. May
twenty-fourth. Where was the Moon? Above us,
shining, cratered and fearless, half no and half yes
blessing us, shining because the Sun said shine,
lighting this night, when even your dirt was divine.

XXXIII.

I want to possess you
the way you possess my mind
all day every day every night
I want be in you
the way you are in me

XXXIV.

I'm a strong man at your feet.
Teach me how to please you.
I'm a big man on my knees
to be the ground beneath you.

Give me strength to hold you up.
I'll do things I'm afraid to:
button down the button-up
and love you when you say to.

Build me up. Break me down.
Leave me all around you.
When my wall falls to the ground,
the broken sound delights you.

I'm a strong man at your feet.
Teach me how to please you.
I'll do things I'm afraid to.
I'll love you when you say to.

XXXV.

In your car we watched the storm grow blue
and moody. Space was charged between us. You said,
The winds inside a storm separate
the charges. One moves toward the ground.

One moves upward. This is the leader.
Lightning seems to move from the cloud
to the ground, but in fact, the ground
has the power. Lightning is a lesson

in physics and humility. Where the
charges are separated, there is
an electric field. Moisture rising.
You're wet, you said. I couldn't speak.

The charge builds up. The electric field becomes
more and more intense. All that is needed
now is a path. The electric field creates
the path. The air around the cloud breaks down.

Before we get ahead of ourselves, you said,
Why do you want to play with lightning? Lightning
is not something to toy with. Tens
of thousands of volts per inch dance on your skin.

Like fire, you said. I pushed against your hand.
All we need is oxygen to burn.
The shortest distance between two points is a straight
line, but the lines of force may not follow.

The lines of force will follow the path of least
resistance. The leader maps out the path
the strike will follow. You touched my throat.
I swallowed hard. The current moves, you said.

God, I said. Yes, you said. God.
The air becomes so hot it explodes,
hotter than the surface of the Sun,
the booming voice of Death rolling.

All of this occurs in a fraction
of a second. Would you like to see it
happen again? You said, Stay in here.
A secondary strike can occur

while the flash from the first is still
visible. Don't stop, I said.
Cloud to ground, ground to cloud, cloud
to cloud, sheet lightning, heat lightning,

ball lightning, red sprites, and blue
jets. Lightning is not something to toy with.
Put your head down, you said. A lightning
rod is simple. It's a low-resistance path.

You said, Sometimes a cage can be a shelter.
A leader does not take the straightest path.
Here it comes again. Mmm, you said.
I'm glad that we could have this little lesson.

XXXVI.

Yes I want it.
Wait for me
to ask for it.

XXXVII.

stop.
Don't
I said,

stop.
Don't

top.
bottom to the
Lick me from the

XXXVIII.

You are not so big,
nor is your whisper,
but you move planets.
Even Jupiter.

Sometimes a comet
is shotput round that
Olympian sphere.
There is an exchange.

In the tick of an
angular moment
the God of the Sky
inches to the Sun.

Of course it happens
to us all the time.
A flower. A sigh.
We are moved by small things.

XXXIX.

Your working face
Lashes blackened
Wet lips darkened
bright and scheming
That's my darling

In the evening
smeared and running
sweating begging
choked and cooning
That's my dark one

Your morning face
completely naked
raw and honest
sweet and searching
that's my baby

I love them all
it's hard to pick
If I had to
your morning face
that's my favorite

XL.

The King controls your breath and life, dear girl.
I hear the things you tell the priests. Oh yes.
What you confess to them, they tell to me,
and that is why I've chosen you tonight.

You say that you don't like this but I know
you dream of this with lesser men than me.
So tell me how it feels to serve the King.
You are so strong. The Queen herself would cry.

The Queen cannot submit herself to me,
but you, my darling, have no choice and so
you understand true power in a way
that royal blood will never understand.

I am your God, and this you must confess:
the priests could never ease your dark distress.

XLI.

A walking willow in the woods,
she bends and sways deeper,
small and tall enough to reach
the Sun, my heart. The air

divides in deference to her,
a parting in the hair
of the Earth, and she moves air,
parting my dark doorway.

She likes a watery wood,
a simple place to grow,
to be filled with the water,
to bend to the wind's will.

I know the trees in this wood.
She is unlike all of them.
Her roots are shallow enough
to move and to move me.

I say she's mine but I am
as much hers as any,
my breath lost in following
her down to the water.

XLII.

Three things I learned from sex:

One. There is no such thing as normal.

Two. The greatest gift you can give someone is your undivided attention.

Three. Sometimes when the world disrespects you and spits in your face, it just wants you to fuck it harder.

XLIII.

I masturbate. I can't wait
till date night. Late night
just got off the phone with you.
Can't be alone with you.
The view is nice
on Instagram.
Damn you're fine.
I used your mouth
like it was mine.

I masturbate. She can relate.
She wakes up, takes up
before she makes up.
She's a shaker, a mover,
a lover, a doctor
rocking up like she's been
knocking off tailors
cuss like a sailor
wants me to nail her
every night. Well, all right.

But not tonight.
Plans are tight.
White children
in the black night.
Black children
in the bright lights.
Sometimes it ain't right
and you can't make it right.

I masturbate. It lifts the weight.
The late show starting,
parting ways professionally.
Can I say confessionally-?
I ordered a pizza,
wisdom the least of
my worries.
I'm not in a hurry
to sleep alone.
I'll roll on the phone
even when I'm asleep.
I keep checking your thread,
head wrecked,
waking up late,
sticking up straight
out the gate.
It's a classical state.
I masturbate.

XLIV.

Mississippi rest stop.
Cottonwood and blackjack oak.
A wild kitten, too hungry to fear me.

Who will take me in,
free me from the stillness of always being hidden,
stop pretending I'm not here?

XLV.

The flat of your back
down under the bridge,
you please the Creator,

your knees in the water,
Saint John the Baptist,
a crowning of mallow.

We see God coming,
an egret descending,
black bull on the levee.

A small metal boat
floats in the amnion,
God in the water.

XLVI.

I see you now down by the creek bed,
your shape in the sand, your tears in the current.
River of grief, mourning and loving,
all of life flowing from time before water.

Even my little mark fades on your body.
How does the memory hold what is dearest?
All that has passed now returns to the mountain
inside your heart, your spirit's headwaters.

XLVII.

Every love has a hopeless side.
It gets bruised- just what it wants:
a never ending misconception,
a puzzle of visions.

Say the name. Hear the music.
Love still has a soul,
an inherent resonance,
dark and moaning like an old piano.

The Devil is lurking.
We became artists of the fear.
Foreboding is part of love's chemistry.
You give love and it comes back,

the miracle of a new comfort.
Every puritan is a hedonist,
an uncomely, frustrated love,
the exasperation in the Gospels.

Love constantly reminds you of
its musicality, like the sea.
The woman in the toll booth is crying.
The couple in the airport kiss like saints.

Love is there like a painkiller.
On the cement outside the dive bar
love spills out onto the sidewalk.
The singer gives the song all she's got.

The voice of love takes over.
Love belongs to the music.
The music belongs to love.
The rhythm is everywhere-

obscene, terrible, and desperate.
Murmur what you've learned in books.
Love takes possession of you.
You are part of love's dream.

That is how you leave your mark,
a heart-shaped ring on a cocktail
napkin. You go home with love
and hope it doesn't kill you.

XLVIII.

Someone is mowing in my neighborhood.
We can't leave the world alone.
Everybody wants to know,
what's going to happen when we die?

Do we learn how to love?
Are we free like wild animals?

Maybe it's the rarest of things:
a quiet summer day
with eternity to wonder:
was there life before death?

XLIX.

In my favorite picture, you are
off to see the royal wedding,
on your knees in the hydrangea,
unbecoming of a lady.

Ruler over all my heart and
everywhere my heart's blood goes, you
can't resist a fetching picture,
knowing they won't start without you.

L.

Dear poet, all respect due to you ma'am,
I think your question might be turned around.
Why do I love thee? runs my thoughts aground
and grinds the rocks of reason into sand.
What does the summer grass offer the lamb?
Why in the caves of France are paintings found? -
perhaps the way the wilder songs would sound
before we were compelled to geld the ram.

My ears seem tuned in some same way to you
to make more of your prayerful, keening voice.
My appetites are driven to your mews,
a migrant craving instinct never lost.
The better question then eludes the muse.
The truest answer is I have no choice.

LI.

I say "you" as if I end at my skin.
You have to draw the line somewhere.
Is that you at the back of my eyes?
Is that you in the foyer of my ears?

I draw a line without boundary,
including you and sometimes only you,
stretching light years and dark years
away to the black horizon of ever.

When I say you are mine, I mean
we are us out to the end of all.
Like the void between stars, we are
hardly anything and everything.

LII.

You ask the goddamnedest questions.
There's no end to truth:
The wood behind the paint.
The brick behind the plaster.
The body under the lake.

At last before the throne,
you find you are the authority.
You were built by slaves.
You were written in the blood of the Messiah.
You are an invasive species.

Come into my garden.
I offer you my worst and you thrive.
I never watered you.
Your flesh is sweet poison.
You are fertile as a supernova.

This love is not a gift we give each other.
We each take this love for ourselves:
Searching. Adaptable. Relentless.
Whatever survives is native.
Only resilience is sustainable.

LIII.

We wake in the morning, your name on my lips.
My prayers for grace echo in your mouth.

How could God disapprove of lovemaking?
It seems impossible.

My Gods love when I make love for them.

Kiss me, wet and sweet, cool when everything else is hot.
When we make love we are gods creating the fecund world.

We choose life. We make life. We take life.
We recreate our shadows again and again.
We conceive ourselves and our filth is immaculate.

The shadow is everything that we're not willing to make conscious.

We come to each other broken, with our little deaths and bones, and we feed each other la petit mort.
We devour each other. These little deaths bring us to life, sharing energy exponentially.

We see the small and holy light in the void and we know the void is holy too,
with its own electricity and convection,
a cycle of life-making perfect in its plan.

I want to create this new life with you.
I want to fuck myself into you,
With seed and sacrifice.
We warm a new planet with our breath
and our sweat, the first rain.

The potential is undeniable. This love is lightning!,
the current of life in a primordial pool

Yes! I scream into the storm
Not afraid
Not anymore
All the little fuckers fucking
I will be the lighting
Every organism driven by life and love and joy and darkness
Fuckers fucking
Fucking fucking fucking little organisms cumming and moaning and keening and praying
Driven by desire
DESIRE, you fucking genius!

We deny desire at our own peril.
We fulfill desire at our own peril.
Like lightning: essential and deadly.
Risk it or die.

Baby, yes! Life came from the choice to say, Yes.
To die spiritually, the death before death, when we deny our desire.
Say YES YES YES Yes

My body misses yours.
Grief. Grieved. Yearning.

I will console you like a storm.

Oh!

The wind brings down the dead branches.

Then shhhhhhhh... like the sound of rain

LIV.

She likes to watch me wash the dishes.
I like when she gets what she wishes.
Sometimes she leaves on every light.
I like what she likes.

She likes to have me in for dinner.
She says that I'm just a beginner.
That's why we practice every night.
I like what she likes.

She likes some things that make me nervous
but I like to be of service.
If she hurts me, that's all right.
I like what she likes.

She likes to make me ask permission
but it's always her decision.
What can I do? My hands are tied.
I like what she likes.

LV.

Your body contains the mind of God.
Its hinges are holy. Its stories are true.

Use it like a map, a compass, and sword,
paradise restored in the blood of the moon.

Memory is food. Sex is survival.
The heart is the headmaster's garden.

For God so loved your body,
the light and the dark were made to contain it.

LVI.

She said, I don't know
if you're my guy
but you're the guy
I'm fucking tonight.

He said, Okay,
but so you know,
I'm devoted to you.
I take good notes.

She said, Do you think
I love you? He said,
Yes. She smiled like
an assassin.

He said, You are made
of stars. You can't help
but burn. Your desire is a
natural force, derived from

from the laws of the Universe
which I cannot abolish
to institute a new Universe
with a God of my authoring.

She said, Are you done?
He said, Be nice to me.
She said, I most certainly
will not. He said, See?

You do love me.

LVII.

Dogwood winter
You love transition
like any clinician
Dr. Feel Something

Ice or fire
begin with Desire
find the center
then go to the edge.

LVIII.

You're no rabbit hunter.
You cry like a big girl
your fear-organ wounded
by intense pleasure.

In the darkness you pray.
You say, Take it. It's yours.
Any good hunter knows
the end is the beginning.

LIX.

Discover dark energy.
A man touches the untouchable.
A woman shares her secrets.
Saturn, visible this night
among the most beautiful cold deserts
as fragile as rainforests.

When I was a child
Mars had no moons.
The God of War was
old truck red.
I hadn't thought to ask
whether the Universe would
tear itself apart.

Here we are, digging deeper,
beauty over flight,
thrilling in the hunt.
Of course dinosaurs had feathers.
Immortality denies evolution.
We're here to do the dirty work,

unlock the secrets of desire,
blow the balloon up, and
watch everything get farther apart.
Don't forget your guide
to the dark side.
Map the wilderness
with the heat that remains.

LX.

It's a nice night. Eighty five degrees. Altair is shining like a flashlight at the other end of the warehouse. I miss the ocean but more I miss the ocean's sky. Atlas himself couldn't have lifted the whole map of the stars.

I'm sweating. The air is thick down low, a warm fog rolling in from the cow fields around. Above the house there's a hole. The great briny ink of the Milky Way boils with living worlds like ours.

There should be a planet where they fall in love once a day. Out of all the planets, surely one would be kinky, or just forgetful. It doesn't have to be someone new every day. I'll fall in love with you hourly.

I'm only looking at the stars because you're not here. The stars are the next best thing. Here in the suburbs, there's a lot of light pollution but I can see well enough to know: there's a place for us.

LXI.

Like a weed you were planted
in poor soil and thrived
Look at you now
so fertile the bees
tongue the hum of your hive
your seeds in the air
your smell by the stairs
Now I am only
an amateur astronomer
but to me you are like
an exploding star
such beautiful trouble

LXII.

The path into the woods
the garden bed
secrets in the shed
snakes in her head

We burn the city
We find the Moon
in the creek
a tunnel to heaven

She calls me like
a house on fire
books in the river
a galaxy on edge

it's hard to tell
just by looking
how I can fit
in tight places

LXIII.

You, harnessed, priestlike
or Athena yet
in her dark disguise,
Grecian lover wed
to battle, oxblood
and nickel steel ringed,
less a motherhood
than a mastering.

Love me yes but not
too much, for I think
you know best the spot
to touch on the brink
of myself and you,
my mind and your will,
a lens to shine through.
The light-like tears spill.

Kiss me bold goddess,
though I know it is
not your way to grace
men of peace like this.
My mission is yours:
to take you inside
the high temple doors
where, unknown, Love hides.

LXIV.

What is love in a land free of towns
no shoes echo in the schoolhouse hall
no one hangs in shame or hunger
none to judge the untamed death

our eyes eggs of visions yet
the will a wilderness to wander
the skin a last defense of all
the heart the smallest living sound

LXV.

Sometimes when we make love
you make me feel like
a frog crossing the road:
an outwitted opponent,
tender and delicious,
and very very lucky.

LXVI.

We go together like blood and whipped cream,
a nightmare and a sweet dream
A baby girl can be a Queen.

All we need is a close shave and a tight rope,
a graveyard and high hopes.
Good and bad are just allotropes.

Please don't stop now- it's a yellow light
Code red to bone white
the Sun sets and suns rise

We tell the truth now no one's watching
in the lusty darkness touching
in an honest trouble trusting

Skin to skin in the bodies apart,
a drum beats in your sweet heart
A seed settles in the deep dark

A seed settles in the deep dark

LXVII.

Whenever I see
a message from you
I hold my phone
like a poker hand.
I suppose I could wait
but this is the truth:
I let you inside me.
That's hard for a man.

I'm not ashamed.
I'm a tactical man.
Hard as it is
I let you inside.
Whenever I hold
a poker hand
I think of my phone
and the aces it hides.

LXVIII.

A tablecloth and a typewriter:
that's my kind of picnic.

What draws you to the stars?
Let me get dressed.

Let's talk about desire.
Wait. Before you leave,

I want to show you Venus.
Meet me in the woods.

Meet me in the full moon.
Unbutton this button.

Will you try something new?
I'd like you to meet someone.

In the cottage in the garden
we can try on these selves.

Be still for a moment.
I want to take a picture.

It's not a typewriter
but it does tells a story.

LXIX.

Because of inflation,
the sexual position
with equitable licks
is now ninety-six.

LXX.

When I wake in the night
I turn myself toward her
It's safe to sleep in church
but you should face the altar

LXXI.

And now I disagree with myself.
I said I had no choice but here we are.
We choose love. Sometimes it needs our help
to navigate when smoke blacks out the stars.

The soul, reborn in fire, sits at the feet
of wisdom. Do we have the will to heal,
the nerve to take the bitter with the sweet,
the faith to go by touch until we feel?

The Sun comes through the trees and turns to sugar.
The sugar fed the fibers of this page.
I offer you not love, but something bigger,
devotion growing stronger at each stage.

The fire is a beginning and an end.
An old tree falls and light comes streaming in.

LXXII.

Witness, surrender.
You have no power.
That is your power:
compassionate love.

LXXIII.

I lost my faith.
It did me a favor, dis-
couraging as it was
to be disgraced before
the god of my mother.

You couraged me
to this grace, this place,
this body remembered,
this perfect alignment-
if anything is perfect,
surely it's this mess.

You like my confidence.
Maybe I'm reckless
to jump in like this.
Maybe I'm dancing
and the organ is playing
Rock of Ages, but this time
I've got nothing to hide.

LXXIV.

I worship at the temple with my mouth.
I sing like an animal. The walls
shake. The roof burns. The Goddess is pleased.
The Goddess says, Please. Here is the key

to all doors. On all fours I come
humble, hopeful, rope around my heart.
My tongue wags hymns and hers meets mine
mumbling clearly needing more of my song.

Wrong. My song needs her, fangs and fur
stirring in the need for a master.
Faster, she says, and I sing faster.
Lower, she says, and I go below her.

There is no way into her more sacred
than the next. Her body is the text.

LXXV.

You fasten the hasp.
Love, like leather, darkens with age.
How does an animal write a poem?
There are no words in the whip.

I twist in my cuffs.
Love, like leather, softens with age.
You are the Goddess.
You are the wordless question.

If you become darker,
I will become softer.

LXXVI.

I want to drive
out of this town
holding your hand
find a quiet
place to be loud

We can be free
enslave each other
We can be pious
to a god unknown

LXXVII.

To the rivers they come, old men,
them potent in the holy world,
to judge the wicked. Papa,
what did they do? Quiet, he says,
This is the way it's always been.
If you sin, you will suffer the same.

In a dream, he drowns me. He prays through his tears.

Tell all pharaohs to
let my people go.

I saw him in Heaven, robed in cold
light, no death to comfort him.
Papa, did you see? I forgave my
body for wanting. Nay, needing.
At the service I spat the sacrament
into the choking reeds, the scarred
hands of Christ around my neck.

Tell all pharaohs to
let my people go.

This is what I get for silence:
your conditional memory,
a monument to cruelty that felt
like love. Once I asked for love
that felt like cruelty, my cries
sang not with death, but with life.
I found evil more forgiving.

Tell all pharaohs to
let my people go.

LXXVIII.

in your dark places
the cold forbidden moon shines
when the Sun goes down

LXXIX.

She's a high brow
in a low heel.
The scene seems slow
how she wows by.

Librarian
around thirty,
dirty minded
Divinity,

I'm good just to
walk behind her
watching her grind
men into dust,

hard as roof tacks.
Lo! The storm breaks.
she throws a rose
in the cruel air.

No mystery
to me at all,
she's a small cat
with a wee purr.

Her sharp claws leave
little love marks,
lifeless larks left
where she sees cause.

Girl's got to eat.
She licks her lips.
Leave a tip, sir,
you and me, too.

LXXX.

I see you
I need you
hand to my heart
mouth open like
a fish eye
so it all fits
in me like a hook
cut me open
there's a ring inside
left by a man
who learned his lesson
to give up control
and live forever
in the soft folds
of your holy book

LXXXI.

Sometimes a risk
will make your safety
seem dangerous.

From inside you,
it sounds like a siren.
Go to your death.

Bring love a sword.
Lay down on a gravestone.
Blindfold yourself.

You are the lamb,
and you have the power
to talk to God.

LXXXII.

He's making a list
and checking it twice
Santa loves naughty girls

LXXXIII.

Every day with you is this holiday,
this holy day to celebrate the birth
and rebirth of the natural year,
green as the wood where I hunt you,
white as the flame of desire,
and red as the blood of your body,
that darkness giving birth to the
light of the God-bearing Goddess.

Before the tree was even up,
we imagined us beneath it,
our dark gifts to each other
all lit up, wrapped in a bow,
the evergreen bondage of
the spirit of giving, the giving
of spirit, and the god-ness of us.

LXXXIV.

Death blooms in the desert.
Bones like the moon flower
high in the windless waste.

The black sky yawns around
but for the hearts of stars
beating low in their graves.

In all this, you touch me.
Your body comes to life
under my fragile lips.

Suddenly, the nothing
opens to allow me.
The door asks, Is this home?

There is very little
but there is just enough.
We join in death's garden,

a headstone for our bed,
fertile ground for the few
lucky enough to live.

LXXXV.

Kings are wicked, and so are you.
You smile sweetly like a paperwhite.
Ah, faith! My neck is slender.

This adventure is a sweet war.
The warm prey tightly in the harness.
Ah, power! Power is seductive.

The world is wicked, and so are you.
Consciousness, the fleshly predator,
slender stethoscopes are your legs.

God, death! Your starry eyes:
faith, life, and death in the firmament,
A survivor is beautiful, just like you.

LXXXVI.

all of nature argues against
the most majestic architecture
all slave to the second law

how unlike that disappointing world
this death-defying love like
a high-dive into the everafter

it's something like immortality
after countless reincarnations
the deathlessness of nirvana

if only for a moment as you
give yourself to me and I
rule you, a king and his kingdom

the Sun and the Moon shine on
a little used planet, the salesman
cries everything must go

the lovers in room three oh one
squeeze in one more forever
just before late checkout

LXXXVII.

John Watts Young was an astronaut
who snuck a sandwich into space
Rye crumbs drifted through the cabin
into life-support equipment

I wonder if he ever thought
to make love in a public place
I always wanted to ask him
Was the risk itself delicious

In the restroom of the museum
people waiting outside the door
I smuggled myself into you
You watched yourself in the mirror

The astronaut? I can't be him
but I know what he did it for
He took a chance like lovers do
Passion lives right next to terror

LXXXVIII.

You're such a slut
You're such a goddess
You're so much of both
you make them the same

Imagine Athena
as a young soldier
in a tent with Telemachus
howling like a cat with her
owl-grey eyes clawing at him
smelling like wine and beef
leaving him no choice but
to take her as she demands

You're such a slut
You're such a goddess
You're so much of both
you make them the same

LXXXIX.

I have a long way to go
all things are made of atoms
some hard and some soft
like books in a foreign tongue

attracting each other
created in the hearts of stars
contempt, desire, and curiosity
in perpetual motion

Finally we now know
like burglars and thieves
the power of the atomic idea
the weight of a flying bird

Some part of our body
like a crowd at a football game
an enormous number of universes
and the opportunity for solitude

the atoms in the apple
like a crossword puzzle
the image of the god
the odor of violets

The Theory of Everything
the pressure of your breasts
the poet in a glass of wine
sorted according to size

It must be dark to see clearly
standing at the seashore
unbidden but persistent
like the wind, invisible

XC.

I bring you roses
as if to a funeral
the veil so mysterious
the skin so ephemeral

I sink like the Sun
into your horizon
We blacken and burn
like all of her citizens

The aquifer swelling
to fill the buds out
now darkens this heaven
where we can take root

XCI.

In the dark we grabbed a hold of some stronger part
of the connective tissue of the universe, a wormhole
between souls, a shortcut through the expanse
that divides everyone's internal experience

knowing it's forbidden to cheat the speed of light
maybe darkness is faster where children hide together
in the space under the bed, where the only light is laughter
and the hot breath like an incubator for wonder

space, the drapes drawn around the stars
that peek between the blankets of our fortress.
Love is risk. We go into the darkness together
where we would never go alone, the space expanding

to hold what is now. The darkness itself is energy,
the underside of everything, the fertile house of
God, the warm heartbeat of the mother Sun cooking
in her bright kitchen, unaware of our secret kiss

XCII.

baby girl! Come here,
dressed like a no no.
You wanna play dirty?
You wanna say Daddy?

Every girl wants to
get to know the Devil
eventually.
Consensually.

You bedevil me
with little white buttons,
blush pink and handcuffs.
There's a red moon soon up.

Use you or lose you.
Touch where only
I can. Open
the old wound
until it blooms
like a flower,
the power that
baby girl has
to get softer.

Daddy gets darker.
What baby girl wants,
baby girl gets,
dressed like a no no.

XCIII.

I have these marks on my back
I hugged a hive of honeybees
I still feel the sting but
the thing was so sweet

Any man can see why
they're willing to die

for their Queen

XCIV.

She said, Are you going to eat it
like a cupcake?

He said, I'm going to eat it like a persimmon cupcake with maple frosting.

She said, That sounds exotic.

He said, It's all-American baby. Just like you.

XCV.

I'm amazed
when you walk
when you breathe
in my ear

You're alive
You're in love
You offer
your body

I take it
like a man
like a saint
on his knees

before God and offers
the One who a body
is not male made of stars
or female made of mud

of desire
of the young
to burn hot
to die old

out of breath
belonging
to someone
to something

beautiful
powerful
and aroused
when you move

XCVI.

She takes the dry dead
roses from the vase,
the old leaves falling
on the countertop,
crackling to the floor
like when she left the
door open on a
late October day.

She pulls crow-footed
petals from their pale
hinges, page after
page in her journal
of love: the bathroom
in the museum. The
roof in Savannah.
The chocolate-dipped
raspberries in bed.

She runs the hot tap
in the old iron tub
and casts the petals
adrift in the sea
where they live again,
warm on her body,
each one a kiss, a
bruise from a heated
moment lost in time,
beyond her recall
but for this language
of miracles, poor
Lazarus rising
from a watery
tomb, a watery
womb where she sings low
and raises the dead.

XCVII.

In the morning
the world turns toward the Sun
I turn toward you

XCVIII.

She said, I've certainly never met a man like you.

He said, And you never will. You better hold onto me.

She said, Well, I'm working on my knots.

XCIX.

I read somewhere
that nuclear fusion
is next to impossible.

Even in the Sun
so many billions of
loves go unrequited,

where the Sun is as dark
as your dreams. Though
the odds are against it,

two protons come
close enough to feel
that life can be bigger.

Across the great void,
the blue eye of an ocean
blinks in the blinding

light of small chances,
enough to make out
two lovers awakening

with a fire so hot
it seems impossible.
Given enough time,

in absolute darkness,
however improbable,
love is inevitable.

C.

I said a year or a hundred poems,
and here it is. It's both-
some magical coincidence
or the power of the oath.

It's morning here and early.
I'm writing in the dark,
remembering this kid I saw
on spring break at the park,

a pale and freckled ginger with a
motion sickness patch
in line to ride the Dragon's Tail, which
he could barely watch.

The park was filled with other thrills-
the Wiley Wheel, the Drop-
but nothing like the Dragon's Tail's
deadly double-loop.

Sun-screen slathered, metal-mouthed,
overgrown, underweight,
perhaps he dreamed he'd fly away
if he could tame this brute.

He pulled the bar across his lap
and gave a nervous look
up to the attendant as the
whole contraption shook,

his summer changed forever just for
having faced this test.
Once you know what's possible,
you can never settle for less.

Then with a whoosh the villagers
were scooped into the Sun!
Clackety-clack the dragon snapped
up the white backbone!

Then it plays a wicked trick
that makes your high heart drop.
Just when you are about to fall,
it hangs you at the top.

You have around five seconds there
to contemplate your choice,
to tease your little sister, or for
her to brave her face.

I couldn't see the young knight but
I know just how he felt,
being by his own will dropped
into the jaws of death.

Explain the cause of such desire.
Explain your lover's touch.
How can one utter anything?
Then, how to say enough?

Forever has to fit inside such
tiny spaces. Yet
the biggest thrill, when things are tight,
is trying to make it fit.

The car blew back into the station,
seeming much too fast.
His hair was wild. His face was red.
The former self was lost.

C. *(continued)*

I recognized within my self
this need I can't explain.
He wanted then, as I do now,
to do it all again.

Ambition is a world with an
orbit of its own.
Desire is more than wanting.
It's a place where we belong.

A year ago, a winter in my soul
turned into spring.
A hundred birds were hatched, and dreamed
of flight, and grew their wings.

I took a chance. I said it so that
I would not back down
and besides, without a deadline,
a book is never done.

Here's a year and a hundred poems-
We'll see how well it ages.
Devotion in its final form
is far beyond these pages.

Jonathan Byrd is a stargazer, songwriter, poet,
fine art photographer, and North Carolina native.
Devotion is his second book.

MEZCALITA PRESS

An independent publishing company dedicated to bringing the printed poetry, fiction, and non-fiction of musicians who want to add to the power and reach of their important voices.

www.ingramcontent.com/pod-product-compliance
Lightning Source LLC
Chambersburg PA
CBHW030901170426
43193CB00009BA/703